THE FORGIVENESS PARADE

also by Jeffrey McDaniel:

Alibi School

The Splinter Factory

The Forgiveness Parade

Jeffrey McDaniel

Manic D Press
San Francisco

for my brother Jon

Cover design: Scott Idleman/BLINK
ISBN-13: 978-0-916397-55-5

Library of Congress Cataloging-in-Publication Data

McDaniel, Jeffrey, 1967-
   The forgiveness parade / Jeffrey McDaniel.
   p. cm.

ISBN 0-916397-55-6
I. Title.
PS3563.C3537 F6 1998
811'.54--ddc21
                              98-25399
                                CIP

CONTENTS

Holding a dying creature during childhood will leave
the offender with trembling hands for life.

> — *from Tell the Bees... Belief, Knowledge,*
> *and Hypersymbolic Cognition, an exhibit*
> *at the Museum of Jurassic Technology*

PART ONE

PART ONE

SURVIVOR'S GLEE

I strapped on an oxygen tank and dove
into the past, paddling back through the years,

emerging from a manhole on memory lane.
The boondocks were doing just fine without me.

The car dealerships. The trash heaps. The stream
of consciousness where I learned how to skinny-dip

had slowed down to a trickle of amnesia.
All the houses had been gutted, except mine,

where my family was still eating dinner. My parents
welcomed me with opened elbows. My brother

looked up to me like a cave drawing on the ceiling.
The night hobbled by, rattling its beggar's cup.

A pipe burst behind my eyes, which brought out
the plumber in everyone. At a loss for words,

I placed a seashell on my tongue, and my relatives
wore bathing suits when they spoke to me.

HOSTILE PROCTOR

The only thing I remember about my mother
and the third grade is the afternoon she wasn't there

when I got off the train. After a thousand shoes
shuffled by, I asked a pair of penny loafers

for a dime and punched out the number. The phone
rang and rang like a slapped cheek. A hundred

briefcases swung past. I tightened my face
and sailed the thirteen city blocks without her.

I pressed the doorbell, like gum into a bastard's
skull. She appeared, clutching a wine glass

like a passport, a tiny black suitcase under each eye.
I peppered that pathetic pink nightgown

with curse words, until she chased me up the stairs,
swinging a wire hairbrush. Later, I called Dad

at the office to complain, but no punishment came,
and after that, I walked home alone every day.

WHERE BABIES COME FROM

For my eighth birthday
I got a toy train set
my father helped assemble.

My job was to hand him
pieces of track and re-light
the cigarettes that went out

in his mouth. Halfway
through, I asked him
where babies come from.

He told me that eight years
ago today I showed up
on the front stoop

in a cardboard box, how
he spent the whole afternoon
putting me together,

just like this train set,
that I was probably lucky
the box arrived on a Saturday.

THE FIRST ONE

Who knows what led me there — a twelve-year-old,
leading my eight-year-old brother and his overnight guest

into the one clean room of that four-story brownstone
and plunging into the booze while our parents slept.

Maybe it was genetic curiosity, colliding with vodka,
a fifth of cheap Russian, and scorching a freeway to our guts,

as we quivered on the oriental rug, passing the bottle
beneath the fancy paintings that held the walls up.

Consequence was a planet whose orbit we couldn't respect.
When the clear stuff got finished, red wine came next,

with little bits of the cork I wedged down with a knife
bobbing like chaperones forced to walk the plank.

The room began flipping like a pancake. We dropped
glass anchors from that third story porthole,

transforming the neighbors into a frenzy of phone calls.
Who knows what emotions my parents were wearing,

but whatever they said didn't make any sense,
as we wiped our lips and spiraled into black.

MANNEQUIN COMPLEX

During my formative years,
my mother had this annoying habit
of taking me into shoe stores
and forgetting all about me.

She'd try on heels and pumps,
sandals and beige leather boots,
winking at herself in the mirror,
like she was Cinderella.

I'd crawl into the stockroom
behind the stacks of boxes,
until the last employee clicked
off the lights and headed home.

Then I'd emerge, place a shoe horn
in the palm of my favorite mannequin,
and sleep at her feet gleefully
because she was my flesh and blood.

BROKEN TOY CLUB

The years begin to show more of his forehead,
where the creases deepen into wrinkles,

and with his three packs a day, a cough
like a goat being skinned alive, it won't be long

before I have to pick up the phone and make
arrangements. There's so much to say,

but as he rattles the ice in his Bombay
and tonic, the only words that fit in my throat

are designed to hurt. With each sip, his eyes
brighten until they shine like flashlights

onto our past. As a child, he held me on his lap,
planted words in my ears that later bloomed

in my mouth. Then the seeds stopped,
and I blamed myself, and when that failed,

I blamed him, performed a nightly Sun dance
with my tongue. *Daaad* became a bell I rang

to remind him to be ashamed for the skyscraper
of dishes in the sink, the banana stains

on the ceiling, the weeks of dog turd in the yard,
while his wife perfected her script of white

wine and downers. Now, half-cocked,
in the same bar she used to wobble out of

like a loose hood ornament, he wants to lay
twenty-five years of dirty socks on the counter.

I could apologize for the seasons of carving
words into weapons and lining him up

for target practice, say *that's kerosene*
under the bridge. You did your best.

But the mercenaries I hired to obliterate
my feelings return, with venom

on their breath, and I launch a *fuck you*,
for old time's sake, at the bull's-eye on his chest.

UNCLE EGGPLANT

When I was a teenager,
my parents would go away
and stick me with the job
of watching blind Uncle Harry.

I'd buckle him in the front
seat of my Chevy Nova
and take him with me
on drug runs into the city.

Okay, Har, you wait here —
I'm gonna dash into this flower
shop and pick up the azaleas.
One day, I returned to the car,

and Harry was gone. I sped
home, placed an eggplant
on his pillow, and told my
parents *I found him this way.*

THE DOLL HOUSE

When my uncle died,
it was decided
to build a doll house
out of his bones.

After some hot water
and lots of scrubbing,
we were ready.

With my sister and I
perched at either shoulder
and an army of screws,
Dad began to build.

A sense of calm came
over the family and
hovered there, smugly.

It was like Christmas
all over again,
only this time
no one got spanked.

THE OBVIOUS

We didn't deny the obvious,
but we didn't entirely accept it either.
I mean, we said hello to it each morning
in the foyer. We patted its little head
as it made a mess in the backyard,
but we never nurtured it.

Many nights the obvious showed up
at our bedroom door, in its pajamas,
unable to sleep, in need of a hug,
and we just stared at it like an Armenian,
or even worse — hid beneath the covers
and pretended not to hear its tiny sobs.

PART TWO

LINEAGE

When I was little, I thought the word *loin*
and the word *lion* were the same thing.

I thought *celibate* was a kind of fish.
My parents wanted me to be well-rounded,

so they threw dinner plates at each other,
until I curled up into a little ball.

I've had the wind knocked out of me
but never the hurricane. I've seen two

hundred and sixty-three rats in the past year,
but never more than one at a time.

It could be the same rat, with a very high
profile. I know what it's like to wear

my liver on my sleeve. I walk in
department stores, looking suspicious,

approach the security guard, say *What?*
I didn't take anything. Go ahead, frisk me,

Big Boy! I go to funerals and tell
the grieving family *The soul of the deceased*

is trapped inside my rib cage and trying
to reach you. Once I thought I found love,

but then I realized I was just out
of cigarettes. Some people are boring

because their parents had boring sex
the night they were conceived. In the year

thirteen hundred thirteen, a little boy died
who had the exact same scars as me.

THE BAD PILGRIM ROOM

When I misbehaved as a child,
my parents would make me undress.
Instead of spanking me,
they'd paint my rear end red,

then place me in a black cloak,
a tall black hat, shoes with buckles,
and lead me down the basement stairs
to the bad pilgrim room.

POSTCARD FROM THE HURRICANE'S EYE

The airplane wing I float back and forth on
was beginning to feel like a boat
until I remembered the photographs
of what a survivor is supposed to look like.
I get by on a diet of white lumps.
My thermos of sunlight serves me well.
Yesterday I saw your face in some algae
before waving the rescue plane away.

LOGIC IN THE HOUSE OF SAWED-OFF TELESCOPES

I want to sniff the glue that holds families together.
I was a good boy once.
I listened with three ears.
When I didn't get what I wanted, I never cried.
I banged my head over and over on the kitchen floor.
I sat on a man's lap.
I took his words that tasted like candy.
I want to break something now.

I am the purple lips of a child throwing snowballs at a taxi.
There is an alligator in my closet.
If you make me mad, it will eat you.
I was a good boy once.
I had the most stars in the classroom.
My cheeks erupted with rubies.
I want to break something now.

My bedroom is so dark I feel like an astronaut.
I wish someone would come in and kiss me.
I was a good boy once.
The sweet smelling woman used to say that she loved me
and swing me in her arms like a chandelier.
I want to break something now.

My heart beats like the meanest kid on the school bus.
My brain tightens like a fist.
I was a good boy once.
I didn't steal that kid's homework.
I left a clump of spirit in its place.
I want to break something now.

I can multiply big numbers faster than you can.
I can beat men who smoke cigars at chess.
I was a good boy once.
I brushed my teeth and looked in the mirror.
My mouth was a brilliant wound.
Now it only feels good when it bleeds.

THE BILLY IN ME

In 1983, I went by myself to see Billy Idol at the Spectrum in Philadelphia. I was sixteen, wearing tight, black jeans, ankle-high combat boots, eyeliner, and lipstick. He was on stage singing *Eyes Without A Face*, and even though there were fifteen thousand people watching him, I knew, deep down, he was telekinetically acknowledging me as his protégé. I was the young Billy, except I was taller and had more depth.

When the show ended, I headed for the real party — the parking lot. I met a plain-looking, seventeen-year-old boy from New Jersey, who liked to ride dirt bikes. I could tell by the way his eyes sparkled — he could see the Billy in me. We talked for hours, then it started to rain. I didn't have enough money for a taxi. The subway was closed. I asked myself, what would Billy do in this situation? Joe said, "Follow me. I have a car."

While driving home through South Philadelphia, Joe asked, "Have you ever thought of having sex with another man?"

"No," I said. "Have you?"

"No," he said. There was a long pause.

"Are you sure?"

The next thing I knew Joe was spilling his guts all over me, saying I reeked of sex, and he just wanted a kiss. If I'd seen a hint of Billy in him, I would've done it. I would've grabbed him by the ears and been his Philly slut. But he was Joe from New Jersey, and his hobby was riding dirt bikes. I asked him if he got excited looking at other boys in the locker room, if he'd ever been with a woman, if he was alone and depressed. Yes, yes, yes. Joe was very depressed and often thought about suicide. This was becoming way too much.

I told him to drop me off at the corner of my street, so he wouldn't know which house I lived in, so he would go far away and never come back.

As I was getting out, I leaned forward and gave Joe the kiss of his life, sucking his tongue like the last hit on the last joint in the whole world, and then I left him there, all worked up, amazed at the Billy in me.

PLAY IT AGAIN, SALMONELLA

Watching a man vomit on the sidewalk
is like going back to my alma mater,

where I was voted most likely to secede.

I carried white lies so far they changed
colors. I held tantrums in my pocket

a long time, before I actually threw them.

I was born with dynamite in my chest.
Some days I wish the real me would stand up

and shout *table for ten, por favor!*

I'm an emotional cripple, putting
his best crutch forward. My heart is a child

clutching his breath underwater. I know

these buttons don't control anything,
but I push them anyway and pretend.

I'm a card-carrying member of a canceled party.

The sound of my own head being shaved
is my all-time favorite song.

NEVER PROMISE SOMEONE A POEM
for Saren Sakurai

When I promised you a poem, I knew
it would come back to haunt me. Now,

rifling through the fibulas in the closet,
I'm back on the Hotel Amazon's dance floor,

with you and four Sarah Lawrence girls so fine —
my heart starts to ricochet, and a one-legged

shiver climbs the bone ladder of my spine.
We didn't have hips back then, playing hoops

each night, swishing pump fake jumpers,
triple clutch drives over each other's fingertips.

Back then, Jaegermeister was a vitamin; D: part
of the alphabet; and Kamikaze: a viable career.

Then graduation hit like a wrecking ball,
trapping us under an avalanche of punk rock,

our values unraveling like mummies
in a mosh pit. No matter how many roses

we stuck up our noses, we always ended up
smelling the thorns. When the sun lifted,

like a fist punching light into our heads,
we were more than just broke, we were broken.

This poem is a silver bracelet. Each link
represents a turning point in our lives,

as the years pass like a caravan of gypsies,
and we stomp across the bridges

of Europe, waving a spy glass, looking for
the fingerprints of our friends who leaped.

BUYING CRACK AT 3:00 A.M.

The gun was so close to my chest — the bullet
ignited my shirt, blood pouring of out me like luck,

as I stamped out the sparks with my fist.
I woke in a hospital bed, a chandelier of tubes

rising from my face. Hooked up to an IV
and a respirator, I felt like a fish tank, filled

with piranhas and Demerol. Mother sobbed
over me like bad weather. Doctors floated in,

flapping x-rays, singing how fortunate I was,
an inch higher and friends would whisper

towards me at night, parents waving my name
as a warning. I was laid out there for a week,

like a question everyone guessed the answer to.
What was he doing there in the first place? It's true,

I've crawled under most of life's hurdles,
but people look at you funny when they know

you almost died. This isn't a scar; it's a word
crossed out on my chest. This isn't a bullet

in my gut; it's the final period in a chapter
of my life that just won't seem to end.

OPPOSITES ATTACK

I walk on tiptoes, so as not to disturb
the blindfolded elderly couple, sleeping

quietly on the floor. Outside the sky
is the color of a drowned man's face.

The birds are still on strike. The local
children build a snow transvestite.

The trees have rolled up their long sleeves.
They're cousins with the octopus.

I remember packing snowballs in the ice box
and dreaming of beaning sunbathers

in July. I was never good at sunbathing.
I used to climb the fire escape and recline

on the roof's rough blanket at midnight,
pretending the house was a wedding cake,

as I covered my limbs with cooking oil
and offered myself to the moon.

Those were the good cold days, when
a Peeping Tom was worth something,

and a wisecrack got you a swift kick
in the pants. Nowadays you need a Glock

in the glove compartment and a cavalry
of narcotics galloping through your veins,

just to get a cop to spill coffee on you,
and sometimes even that isn't enough.

I'll see your cross-eyed pigeon
and raise you a jar of epileptic brains.

Put your business cards on the table.
Read the palm trees and weep.

Roman orgies weren't built in a day.
I bet you an opera singer's esophagus

that my apocalypse can beat your
apocalypse — even on an off night.

SIAMESE OPPOSITES

I was feeling lonely.
Phones were ringing in my fingers.
I held a light bulb to my sternum in the dark.
My birthday came and went
each night without saying hello.
I sat for hours with a telescope,
gazing into the stove.
Hermits looked up to me.
They piled their beards outside my window.
I was a nation of peasants.
I signed all my checks *Nation of Islam*
and changed my name to Rated X.
My hands were Siamese opposites.
I ate my eggs with a glue stick and scissors.
I pierced my spleen.
I had the word *Galapagos* tattooed on my liver.
I flirted with the wives of nuclear warheads
and nibbled on the tonsils of emperors.
I blew my nose with a napkin signed by Jòan Miro.
Each time I saw God,
He had pantyhose pulled over His face.
I handed out UFOs at all the bus stops.
I walked around holding a big piece of cardboard
and told everyone I was Heaven's Door.

CAFE TROPICAL

It was the kind of weather you'd expect to find
in the mind of a mad woman — rays of sunlight

neatly stacked next to a pile of wind, teenagers
dribbling rain drops the size of basketballs

outside *Sven's Institute of Voodoo & Macramé*,
and across the street a single blanket of snow,

landing impeccably on the back of a banker
on a steam grate. Not bad for the fourth of June,

I thought, as I buttered my toast in a you-scratch-
my-back-I'll-scratch-yours kind of way. The day before

I bought a box of baseball caps, climbed to the roof
of the local skyscraper, tried tossing the hats

onto the heads of office workers eating tofu burgers
on their lunch breaks. Anyhow the way I was chewing

my toast made it sound like I was saying *golf pro,
golf pro, golf pro*, when a squirrel grabbed my tea bag

and disappeared into the tangible curtains
of humidity. *My purse, my purse* I screeched.

STATIONARY EARTH

If the Earth stopped revolving,
it would always be noon

in Manhattan, midnight
in Tokyo, where the alcoholics

would all move to, because
the bars were never closed.

Early birds would flutter
to California, where the day

was always just beginning.
Rich people would take cruises

to watch the sunset, where
drowned lovers would wash-up

like clumps of seaweed —
a person could die of old age

without ever seeing another hour
besides the one he was born in.

Night owl would become a race.
Insomnia: a philosophy. Me?

I'd drift on plywood to that
instant before dawn, where the sky

is a canvas painted by Mark
Rothko, and the moon is as round

as the mouth of a fireman
running out of a burning building.

THE FARMER

There's a field where I grow only bruises,
inner gnawing, and heartache.

Each Saturday I harvest the crop,
haul it to the open-air market, and sell it
straight from my flatbed truck.

Fresh agony only three bucks a bushel.
Sun-dried torment by the pound.

Seven years running, my pain
has been voted best in the region,
and while I'm not wealthy,

in my own small way,
I help keep the village alive.

PART THREE

THE QUIET WORLD

In an effort to get people to look
into each other's eyes more,
and also to appease the mutes,
the government has decided
to allot each person exactly one hundred
and sixty-seven words, per day.

When the phone rings, I put it to my ear
without saying hello. In the restaurant
I point at chicken noodle soup.
I am adjusting well to the new way.

Late at night, I call my long distance lover,
proudly say *I only used fifty-nine today.*
I saved the rest for you.

When she doesn't respond,
I know she's used up all her words,
so I slowly whisper *I love you*
thirty-two and a third times.
After that, we just sit on the line
and listen to each other breathe.

THE SECRET

When you were sleeping on the sofa,
I put my ear to your ear and listened
to the echo of your dreams.

That's the ocean I want to dive in, merge
with the bright fish, plankton, and pirate ships.

I walk up to people on the street
that kind of look like you and ask them
the questions I would ask you.

Can we sit on a rooftop and watch stars
dissolve into smoke rising from a chimney?

Can I swing like Tarzan
in the jungle of your breathing?

I don't wish I was in your arms.
I just wish I was pedaling a bicycle
toward your arms.

ANOTHER LONG NIGHT
IN THE OFFICE OF DREAMS

There's a woman I'm in love with, but I forget
what she looks like, so I take out my paintbrushes
and create my image of her.

Your eyes are blue like the morning of going.
Your ears are tender twists of logic. Your thighs
are impossible avenues my car swerves out of control on.

I want to cut the silence with one of your shoulderblades,
blow moon-shaped kisses to orbit your skull
as you sleep on the highest ledge of my insomnia,

but I'm a broken promise in a pawn shop,
and this is just a secret that happens to involve you.

THE CALLER

I was twelve when the first call came —
no sisters, an all-boys school, a mother

strung out on a horrible clothesline.
It was a wrong number, but the female voice

kept asking questions: *do you play sports . . .*
wear a jock strap . . . what's your cock like . . .

are you touching it now? And just like that
I was hooked, or rather she grabbed

a hook already in me and tugged
me up and down the walls of puberty.

Each week for six years she called
with stories of whacking off married men

on commuter trains, beneath the leather
jacket she draped on their laps.

It was as if she climbed from the pages
of the porno book stashed under my bed

just to whisper *I want to fuck you*
in a room full of blind people, in the back seat

of a cop car during a high speed chase.
High school girls couldn't compete

with her narcotic whimpers, as she dipped
the phone to the vibrator's chain saw.

Ten years later, walking up 18th Street,
I realize there's something incredibly

honest about trees in winter, how
they're experts at letting things go.

PORNOGRAPHY FOR EUNUCHS

Masturbating is too much like patting
yourself on the back. I'd rather carve

my social security number into oak trees.
In the forest of high heels, I'm always

barking up the wrong thigh. Do you
believe in ambivalence at first sight?

I was arrested by your beauty, but not
convicted. I'm so horny I could lick

a pair of panties through a washing
machine. My Alcatraz bone is bruised

and muted. If a touch dies on a thigh,
what do you wear to the funeral?

Have you ever had such great sex
you forgot what language you spoke?

Perdon, necesito to cover myself
with leeches and pretend I'm at an orgy.

It's hard not to smell the Vatican coffee
after it's been dumped on you by God.

THE FIASCO IN COLORADO

I wish I could blame it on the Halloween negligee
you stripped down to the first night our lips

smashed, or the oxygen we exchanged under
a tangled necklace of stars, skirt rising like a silk

curfew. I wish I could blame it on the Flamenco
dance that was your bed, the secrets carefully

positioned like abstract paintings we lacked
the vocabulary to discuss, or the fiasco in Colorado,

when you glistened on the dance floor,
and all the men stared at you, like a bright idea

they were having together, as opiates eroded
in my bloodstream, and a red-eye flight

crashlanded in your arms. Lascivious gaga,
tornado hips, every minute my thoughts glitter

back to you, God punches in the holy digits
and shoves me back two, because your carwreck

kisses left me with whiplash, and I still haven't
washed your lipstick from my neck brace.

THE JERK

Hey you, dragging the halo —
how about a holiday in the islands of grief?

Tongue is the word I wish to have with you.
Your eyes are so blue they leak.

Your legs are longer than a prisoner's
last night on death row.

You're a dirty little windshield.

I'm standing behind you on the subway,
hard as calculus. My breath
sticks to your neck like graffiti.

I'm sitting opposite you in the bar, waiting
for you to uncross your boundaries.

I want to rip off your logic
and make passionate sense to you.

I want to ride in the swing of your hips.

My fingers will dig into you like quotation marks,
blazing your limbs into parts of speech.

But with me for a lover, you won't need
catastrophes. What attracted me in the first place
will ultimately make me resent you.

I'll start telling you lies, and my lies will sparkle,
become the bad stars you chart your life by.

I'll stare at other women so blatantly
you'll hear my eyes peeling,

because sex with you is like Great Britain:
cold, groggy, and a little uptight.

Your bed is a big, soft calculator
where my problems multiply.

Your brain is a garage
I park my bullshit in, for free.

You're not really my new girlfriend,
just another flop sequel of the first one,
who was based on the true story of my mother.

You're so ugly I forgot how to spell!

I'll cheat on you like a ninth grade math test.
Break your heart just for the sound it makes.

You're the *this* we need to put an end to.

The more you apologize, the less I forgive you.

So how about it?

HUNTING FOR CHERUBS

If you heard your lover scream in the next room, and you ran in and saw his pinkie on the floor in a small puddle of blood, you wouldn't rush to the pinkie and say *Darling, are you okay?* No, you'd wrap your arms around his shoulders and worry about the pinkie later. The same holds true if you heard the scream, ran in, and saw his hand, or, God forbid, his whole arm. But suppose you hear your lover scream in the next room, and you run in, and his head is on the floor, next to his body, which do you rush to and comfort first?

WINTER LANDSCAPE WITH MANATEE

Imagine my surprise when I saw her, a manatee,
one of the world's endangered species,
floating on the surface of my bed. Columbus
saw a manatee in the Caribbean and called it
a mermaid. I'll call this one *Caballero*.

Caballero, I feel like we've met before.
Maybe our parents took us to the same movie
when we were eleven and left us alone in the lobby
where we exchanged an awkward glance.

If I was God, I'd make flowers
smell like the back of your neck,
trees with trunks as soft as your thighs.
A bird is just a prayer with wings.
But I am not that blue the sky was
when I woke in the harbor of your arms.

The next day I looked at the imprint
our bodies left in the snow
and remembered a fireplace with limbs,
a Japanese lantern with lips.

It was more than just the cold stuff, melting
through my jeans, that made my spinal column
tremble like a xylophone. No, our outline
doesn't resemble a snow angel,
but it makes me feel like I'm related to one.

LETTER TO THE WOMAN WHO STOPPED
WRITING ME BACK

I wanted you to be the first to know — Harper & Row
has agreed to publish my collected letters to you.

The tentative title is *Exorcist in the Gym of Futility*.

Unfortunately I never mailed the best one,
which certainly was one of a kind.

A mutual friend told me that when I quit drinking,
I surrendered my identity in your eyes.

Now I'm just like everybody else, and it's so funny,
the way monogamy is funny, the way
someone falling down in the street is funny.

I entered a revolving door and emerged
as a human being. When you think of me
is my face electronically blurred?

I remember your collarbone, forming the tiniest
satellite dish in the universe, your smile
as the place where parallel lines inevitably crossed.

Now dinosaurs freeze to death on your shoulder.

I remember your eyes: fifty attack dogs on a single leash,
how I once held the soft audience of your hand.

I've been ignored by prettier women than you,
but none who carried the heavy pitchers of silence
so far, without spilling a drop.

THE WOUNDED CHANDELIER

I went into a bar and ordered a childhood dream.
A woman came in and sat down next to me.

She was rather lanky for an amputee.
A voice said *she's too shallow to dive into.*

You'll break your noose on her concrete psyche.
I didn't listen. As a way of shattering the ice,

I told the story about the hemophiliac
who went bungee jumping, how his body

was this delicate sack of blood, bouncing
up and down in the air. I found myself

whispering things like *I only have eyebrows
for you.* She asked me to take her home.

I carried her promises up the stairs.
They were as fragile as lightbulbs.

I was gonna defy gravity in her celestial body,
but I had performance anxiety so I wrote *Baby*

Jupiter in black magic marker on her forehead
and plummeted back into the bar.

ORBITED BY KISSES

She's the only one in the coffeeshop,
and I can't tell her apart. With eyes the color

of an ax blade swinging, I can hear
the arguments now. *I never liked you*

in the first place! Is nothing sacred? The truth is
we shared a single clumsy kiss, briefer than cheesecake,

that left my body tingling like a blind man's nose,
because I haven't electrified a woman

in thirty thunderstorms, and her hair is a bucket
of nectar dumped at dawn from a bridge.

Her kisses were better spinning at a safe distance,
holding my neck in a constant state of threat,

and guiding my life with their possibility.
Now she's made herself real and ruined everything.

I guess I'm the one left holding the amaranth.
The halo is first cousins with the noose.

If I had courage, I'd say *you bring out*
the ambrosia in me. But I don't. I have this fear

of her rushing towards me, as if I'm train leaving
a station. She missed me. I'm already gone.

CARACAS

I wish slitting the wrist of the clock
would let this moment last forever —

your tongue so deep in my ear
it feels like a paintbrush, coating

the dark, peeling walls inside my head
with a carmine veneer. I was expecting

you to run, when you saw the cartilage
in the closet. I was prepared to chase

after and whisper *you have beautiful
footsteps*, when the truth is you make

my toes tingle like the capital of Venezuela.
I know loving me isn't easy — the all-night

helicopter parties, the glow-in-the-dark
haircuts, but when I look at you

it's like praying with my eyes. I know
it's stupid to not own a gun yet have

so many triggers, but in some other world
gigantic seashells hold humans

to their ears and listen to the echo
of machines. I apologize for the fossils

growing on the dishes, how the rug is covered
with cocktail umbrellas when you wake up,

but it was raining margaritas, and the stars
came on backwards last night.

ABSENCE MAKES THE HEART GROW FONDUE

On the scales of desire, your absence weighs more
than someone else's presence, so I say *no thanks*

to the woman who throws her girdle at my feet,
as I drop a postcard in the mailbox and watch it

throb like a blue heart in the dark. Your eyes
are so green, one of your parents must be

part traffic light. We're both self-centered,
but the world revolves around us at the same speed.

Last night I tossed and turned inside a thundercloud.
This morning my sheets were covered in pollen.

I remember the long division of Saturday's
pomegranate, a thousand nebulae in your hair,

as soldiers marched by, dragging big army bags
filled with water balloons, and we passed a lit match

back and forth between our lips, under an oak tree
I had absolutely nothing to do with.

PART FOUR

THE WATER IS DROWNING

In a strip club, the optimist only stares
at the bright side of a dancer's ass.

Conversely, who would American poets
seduce without graduate programs

in creative writing? When I lean into
the scent of a tulip, I do not smell

the flower, but the noses of those
who sniffed before me. Then again,

when the face of a cheating husband
dissolves in a wedding picture, what can

a good Samaritan do, but masturbate
backwards on a child molester's grave?

LEONARD

The boy was bright, like the retarded girl
he set on fire. No one predicted
she'd ever be so understood. Death
has a way of making sense out of everything.
Take that mother in New York City
who dragged her daughter down
Avenue B from a '78 Buick's
back fender. Didn't the whole block agree
this was no way to celebrate a birthday?

But who hasn't gotten mad and dreamed
of shining a lit cigarette into someone's ear?
Who hasn't been lonely and fantasized
about covering couples kissing in public
with blankets of kerosene? Like I said,
the boy was bright — perfect scores
on thirty-seven consecutive math tests,
a national chess champ at thirteen —
and Columbus Junior High bored him,

so one Christmas Eve, he set a retarded girl
named Rachel Cleaves on fire
and watched Delancey Street fill with people,
amazed at what they'd done.

FAIRY TALE IN REVERSE

If only we'd planted a black box in your skull,
like the ones dug out of airplane wrecks,

we could've salvaged your last thoughts,
and known, if not why, at least what,

but all we have is a body: the bruised
alabaster of your thighs, make-up so thick

a picnic could sink in it, legs so thin and sickly
they weren't even bones, but diminishing

chimes of hope, and your heart: a time bomb
that took twenty-six years to explode.

GREAT HUMANS

When Hart Crane leaped from the *Oriziba*
all the poems still in his head floated

to the surface of the Gulf of Mexico
where they sparkled like tropical fish.

Sylvia Plath plucked her skull in the oven
because her cranium was packed

with images that were only half-baked.
Houdini could make tattoos levitate.

Sigmund Freud's middle name was *Buck*.
J. Edgar Hoover only wore black bras.

Hitler took the *fun* out of funerals.
We don't have great humans anymore.

We have great drugs. *Proh-zak* sounds like
all your problems being electrocuted.

Meth-am-fet-a-meen sounds like a school bus
your mouth is always late for. Snort

enough cocaine and just watching the sun rise
will feel like a form of plastic surgery.

Heroin is an extremely comfortable shirt,
that hurts when you take it off,

and a junkie is just a vampire, sucking
the last pint of blood from his own neck.

TOUR GUIDE TO THE NATION'S CAPITAL

The Lincoln Memorial must be experienced
at night, preferably the wee hours. Just don't

go on a Wednesday. There's this maniac
with a crowbar, lurking behind the columns.

Legend is he's the ghost of Norman Mayer,
a nuclear protester, shot dead by the cops

in '82 for threatening to blow up
the Washington Monument with explosives

he didn't have. The next place to visit
is the *Exorcist* staircase and the Hilton wall

where Reagan got capped. But don't go
to the White House, unless there happens

to be a cook out, and don't go blind looking
at cherry blossoms either. Instead draw

chalk outlines of your favorite diplomats
outside the Iraqi Embassy, then hail

a taxi to the Watergate Hotel. Pay the driver
with very quiet bills. Don't be alarmed

if the trees are filled with plumbers —
they're looking for the branch that leaks.

RENO

You are the quirky little sister of Las Vegas
that never finished high school, with your Kurt

Cobain slot machine, where instead of apples
and oranges, different brands of pharmaceuticals

revolve in Kurt's head. A pair of valiums
doubles your bet, but three shotgun shells

is the big pay-off. Reno, your pawn shops
are loaded with prosthetic limbs and wedding rings.

One night a lucky bastard cackled down your strip,
chucking twenty-five dollar chips over his collar,

then dumped the whole six thousand in the river
just to watch the panhandlers plunge.

When the moon's right, their femurs still glitter
like rods of gold. I could stay here forever,

whispering the details of the life I left behind
to the blackjack dealer who flicks me my future

one card at a time. The Jack & Gingers stack up
like a glass chimney, as the losers are hauled out

on gurneys, howling for one last chance. Lady
Luck whips out a hag wrench, prying my smile off

one nerve ending at a time, and I wander
the desert at dawn, like a general returning

to his senses after bombing his own people,
muttering *My God, what have I done?*

THE FORGIVENESS PARADE

There's nothing like a full moon, reflected
in the eyes of a blind man, using a telescope

to stir a bowl of Russian alphabet soup
for the cosmonauts, who orbited the shadow

of Jupiter and are landing in an ocean
of tears shed by cold-blooded murderers,

who miss their mothers convulsively
in their prison cells, being wheeled

caravan-style down Oswald Boulevard
as part of the forgiveness parade,

where relatives of the victims stand quietly,
holding banners like *Apology Accepted*,

as the vandals stumble past in shackles,
followed by the hijackers and the pickpockets,

who march single-file up the fire escape
of a skyscraper built by arsons.

POETRY NATION

In the capital square, there is a statue of Jack Spicer,
puking his guts out, his last words — *My vocabulary
did this to me!* — inscribed in the marble base.

In nightclubs, supermodels stomp their heels
and dream of their smal, dark hearts
being enlarged with compassion implants,
as the poetess gets all the attention.

Guys in trendy rock bands mope like damp rats
whenever a poet storms into a room.

Everyone wants to be a poet, even the coroner
scribbling in his note pad at the crime scene:
a drowned man is judged only by his piers.

Carjackers pause in mid-heist to consider the moon.
Hallmark is burned to a crisp. Bill Knott's silhouette
appears on every other thirteen dollar bill.

Homeless people stand in line for Pablo Neruda.
In hospitals, they feed cancer patients Carolyn Forche.
In churches, there are giant wooden replicas
of Emily Dickinson nailed to a cross.

Instead of NBC and CBS, there is W.S. Merwin,
the Walt Whitman channel, and Sappho at Nite.

The Constitution was written by Tristan Tzara.
All men are created equal under Dada.
The drug czar makes sure everyone gets enough.

Lucille Clifton for President!
Charlie Parker is the national bird.
Howl is recited before pro football games.
You can pay for groceries with words.

Jeffrey McDaniel, 30, lives in Los Angeles, California where he teaches poetry writing workshops at U.C.L.A. Extension, and as part of Poets-In-The-Classrooms sponsored by PEN West. He has read his work at the Smithsonian Institution, and on National Public Radio's *Talk of the Nation*. This is his second book.

ACKNOWLEDGMENTS

Thanks to the editors of the following magazines, anthologies, and recordings, where earlier versions of some of these poems previously appeared: *Another Chicago Magazine, Art/Life, Beyond the Valley of the Contemporary Poets, Blue Satellite, Cups, Gargoyle, Gulf Coast, Hawaii Review, Lucid Moon, Meow: Spoken Word from the Black Cat, My Tongue Is A Red Carpet I Only Roll Out For You, New (American) Poets, New Orleans Review, Onyx Anthology, Pearl, Plazm, Ploughshares, Poetry Nation, Sic (Vice & Verse),* and *Walt Whitman's Beard.*

Thanks to Cindy Goff, Thomas Lux, Joel Brouwer, and Silvana Straw for their editorial support; to the D.C. Commission for the Arts for their financial assistance; and my family, Christine Caballero, Ellyn Maybe, Jennifer Joseph, the performance poetry community, D.C. WritersCorps, Beyond Baroque, and many others for their generosity, tolerance, and love.